Like Frost

ON THE

Winter Garden

-An Anthology of Poetry-

Austie M Baird
-Editor Cover Artist-

Austie M. Baird is a born and raised Oregonian, holding both History and Education degrees from Eastern Oregon University. Long before becoming a wife and mother, Baird connected with the power of the written word, finding healing properties in both reading and writing. She draws strength from the beauty that surrounds her and the overwhelming love of her family.

A.B.Baird Publishing
Oregon, USA

Printed in the United States of America

First Printing, 2019

ISBN 978-1-949321-07-4

Cover Art Image by Austie M. Baird

A.B.Baird Publishing
66548 Highway 203
La Grande OR, 97850
USA

WWW ABBAIRDPUBLISHING COM

-TABLE OF CONTENTS-

-DEDICATIONS-

To Elizabeth Bonaiuto (Instagram handle @wordshurtandhealme)
You make my words sure of themselves. As their lightbringer, you are the reason they thrive.
-AMBICA GOSSAIN

For my Instagram family
-MEI RYAN

I would like to dedicate my contribution to this anthology to my Mum -thank you for all that you were and that you gave to me — and to Dean, who is now my home.
-FAY LEE

To my mother,
Who always believed in me.
Who encouraged me to use my talents and follow my dreams.
I know that you watch over me, your love is still a guiding light.
-LIES DE WILDE

To everyone who has loved and encouraged me:
My parents, my students and Franklin Family, all of the Buck's Lake Beauties, Book Club, and to Bob, Dylan, and Drew, who make this life worth living.
-RHONDA SIMARD

To those who helped me grow, through frost & thaw.
-AUSTIE M. BAIRD

AMBICA GOSSAIN

[TRYST_WITH_FICTION]

Ambica Gossain is a flourishing female Indian poet whose following has been well established on Instagram. Although she has been writing poetry for only 2 years, her work has been featured by many renowned Instagram poetry communities such as @herheartpoetry @bymepoetry and @globalwordsmiths. Her writing has been featured in major publications, such as the national daily Hindustan Times and Wedding Affair magazine.

Ambica was raised in Dubai and New Delhi. She earned her Bachelor's degree in Biochemistry at Oberlin College in the United States. She returned to her home country, India, where she draws on her varied experiences and education to imbue a unique perspective to her poetry.

As Director of Customer Relations at Securico, a security systems manufacturing company, Ambica's zeal for getting to know people across the globe was instrumental in making Securico the largest corporation of its kind in India. When she took a short break from work to raise her children, she discovered her passion for writing poetry. She is also a gourmet cook, sitar musician and devoted yoga disciple.

-Our Stories-

We are not just whispers, hushed to conceal, a past averted eyes won't reveal.
Bated breaths of trouble, like air we'll rise, bullets with butterfly wings in a tangle of
fire and ice.
Treading water (thicker than blood) in wishing wells, floating hope on a string of
broken spells;
to write hedonistic lyrics that lie about our wilting innocence in sunsets and starfire.

~ our stories are worth being told.

Ambica Gossain

-Genes-

She is her father's indiscretions;
she is her mother's ignorance.
But she is also a will of titanium and a bastion even the hint of injustice dare not
breach.

~ she is more than her genes.

Ambica Gossain

-Home-

Feet touch back down on uneven exiled ground,
studded with mounds of cow dung fashioned into an unusual obstacle course.
Spiced winds whisked in rambunctious kitchens tickle my nostrils,
before engulfing me in the stench of sewage from their backyards.
The turbine engines are still running making my head want to bolt,
but my heart feels at home, deep down in my conflicted bones,
where I cannot deny that beauty is indeed only skin deep.

AMBICA GOSSAIN

-An Indian Woman-

She's an Indian woman with complexion wheat, jaundiced yellow in spite of the
blistering heat.
Resilient, supple skin, churned of clarified butter; restraining sensual hips, swaying
hearts aflutter.
She's got mud in her bones and grit in her teeth, from working the earth; calloused
hands and feet.
She buried her dreams in cow dung, timber and coal to give flight to yours; their caged
wind she condoled.
Her sacrificial limbs slaughtered to placate the Gods.
Blood, sweat and tear libations to survive the odds.
She is the benevolent bestower and the avenging destroyer, endowed with precipiced
loins; equilibrating karmic sin.
She's the temptress, the scourer of your predatory skin.

AMBICA GOSSAIN

-Fragile Faith-

Cherished leaves of the past pressed between condemned chapters of today,
frequented when fragile faith is pummeled and pried away.
We hold them close to our heart, lest the wind whisks them astray.
Their redolence kindling the flutter of sweet triumph's return some day.
Tired hope, ebbing embers in the wake of raging sparks we've burned right through,
flooding light on the dark.
But I'm going to need you till I breathe my very last, so hang on a little longer;
I promise we'll come back stronger, our blind trust steadfast.

Ambica Gossain

-Skin-

I searched for a higher purpose.
I made the naive presumption that I was made for more,
but what if my only Karma was to accept the skin my soul wore.

Ambica Gossain

-COCKTAIL-

I am many people.
My amorphous identity defended by multi-headed Hindu Gods;
relinquished to the speculative distance between your censorious interpretations and
my own mythical representation.
Each face bespoken to indulge your palate; I am a potent cocktail of stirred spirit selves,
giving you the heady rush you need to swallow me.

AMBICA GOSSAIN

-SINNERS AND SAINTS-

It's not that I couldn't tell right from wrong or black from white or even grey.

My moral dilemma was really just buying me time until degeneration evolved
sufficiently,

subsuming my transgression within its permissible limits, black bleeding into the white.

And with the current state of the world, all I had to do was wait, for a miscreant like
myself to be proclaimed a saint.

AMBICA GOSSAIN

-WRONG ARMS-

His prolonged absence, thick air over the constancy of bone,
haunted the empty frames on the vermillion walls of my hemorrhaging heart.
My countless achievements only succeeded at accruing shadow souls,
as I dejectedly sought validation in all the wrong arms.
Entranced by the faintest allusion to a father figure, I made men out of juvenile boys;
their youth sabotaged by a maturity I couldn't reverse.
But they were better for it and I had managed to stall the clock, just long enough to
catch up.

AMBICA GOSSAIN

-MESSY-

Yearning for more, settling for less,
I pull the trigger, words blowing my brains out instead;
I let poetry clean up the mess.

AMBICA GOSSAIN

-Not Guilty-

I used to cry words.
They were my tears, a gushing torrent draining my fears in verses insincere.
It became all too easy to believe what I wrote and forget what was real.
Then more easy to stop feeling and start denying everything I easily concealed.
But I did it anyway, because I had to find a way to survive, and this was clearly the lesser
evil than the vices my beguiling demons had contrived.
I've got blood on my hands but need not plead guilty on the stand.
My words, an airtight alibi, confer undeniable proof; negating the plausibility of my
villainies with me in the same room.

AMBICA GOSSAIN

-Madness-

To live furled in the crook of the tyrannizing edges of your mouth,
fettered to the capricious dispositions of your labyrinthine mind,
is the cruel and twisted pleasure that begs my indulgence.
Lost in your madness, I am found, in our predilection for a melancholy that begets the
only happiness we recognize.
The kind that's simply a frown turned upside down.

AMBICA GOSSAIN

-PEACE ON EARTH-

Let it all fall away. Let it crumble.
The mountain of expectation casting its foreboding shadow where sunny intentions
should frolic carefree,
vulnerability tethered only to our morality.
Let gratitude come from brazen benevolence,
the unconditional giving of one's soul.
Let me not ask you what you can do for me,
but ask myself what I can do for you instead.
My actions gratuitous, independent of your calculated reaction,
as I circumvent tricks of light and animation;
to shoot love straight from the sterling centre of my unalloyed heart.
The hearth and home of peace on earth within you.

AMBICA GOSSAIN

-NOOSE-

I threw you a lifeline
and you noosed it
to strangle me.

AMBICA GOSSAIN

-LET'S NOT DO THIS-

Let's not do this. Talk about all the things that could go wrong.
Because they will if they must and life is too short for me to chase and too hard for me to face.
Let's live an illusion of happiness, so hard, we believe it to be the truth;
so that the stars are forced to realign themselves with our vision of the way the world should be.
Let's do this. Let's imagine every minute detail of our utopia and make it a reality with the conviction in our hearts.
If for no other reason, simply because this is a better way to live.
This is an easier way to breathe.

AMBICA GOSSAIN

-MELANCHOLIC MARIONETTES-

You weren't expecting the honest admission of my fallibility, the self-victimization of an underdog,
deflecting blame to pin fault on an unknown other's baseness.

You were too distant from the facts to form a judicious opinion,
denying responsibility for my actions by making excuses for who I really was.

I left you reaching blindly into the dark, to manifest a silhouette of what you desperately wanted me to be, needing me to endorse your fabricated sense of security.

You made the active choice to love me without letting the sound of silence reverberate from my many shortcomings, filling endless affirmations of my character assessment.

Because neither of us would risk losing their best friend, not even to my masochistic penchant for starting fires.

It was not my fault; after all, I had a flint lodged in my heart, a wilderness you were content to keep extinguishing among my other unsettling traits.

You had always been the one, swimming tirelessly, sustaining us afloat in my sea of smoke.

And we had come too far to let the weight of our damp wood make melancholic marionettes of us.

AMBICA GOSSAIN

-MORNING-

The first light filters through drawn drapes, scintillating undulations of tender hope
dancing on swollen lids,
holding back tears that threaten to render them impotent every time our lips part.
Those three magic words catapulted into the past, with each grenade's counterattack,
blowing to bits our already slim chance at survival.
But we have this, the meagre minutes before we pump ourselves with caffeine, to brave
each other when we can't face the world.
And I'll use it everyday, this brief reprieve of somnolent silence, to repair what we
broke with our wakeful words.

AMBICA GOSSAIN

-OPIATED ESCAPE-

You dunked me in a glass of water, watched me disintegrate;
then dissolve into something you could stomach, that resembled happiness.
We were the pill you hated but popped anyway;
the illusion you swallowed to get you through yet another day.
I know I need to cure you of this addiction but I'm too afraid
to admit you never truly loved me without the opiated escape.

AMBICA GOSSAIN

-EXPRESSION OF LOVE-

Our expression of love, first forged by the brush of our mother's tender bosom,
nuances sheltered in our father's origami arms.

Its script nipped and tucked by nature versus their ability to nurture is birthed at the
intersection of anticipation and commitment.

And yet when I touched down on foreign ground, your perception of loving me
conflicted with my understanding of being loved.

Susurrations lost in translation, our incompatible words and actions collided; their
dust-filled mirages perpetuating the growing divide between two tied tongues.

~ we never spoke the same language

AMBICA GOSSAIN

-MIRAGE-

The only trouble with loving you, is loving the me that isn't me, loving the you that
isn't you.
Mirage.

AMBICA GOSSAIN

-My Heart and Your Head-

In retrospect, I went about it all wrong, wanting you to see yourself through my eyes;
painting rosy hues where greys resided.

I froze out the demons that needed to be confronted instead, to ensure they'd all either
been slain or had fled.

So that they couldn't thaw their surreptitious way back into the wedge, demarcating
the distance between my heart and your head.

Ambica Gossain

-Heartbreak-

Darling, breathe. I was only ever meant to be a surge on the EKG,
faltering and flatlining into the epiphany that heartbreak is the first brick
in the foundation of your happily ever after.

Ambica Gossain

-Antidote-

You were always the antidote to the venom coursing through my veins.
But I understood my choices: breathing my last or drawing yours.
And you were too exquisite to sacrifice, for a soul the devil had already bargained for.
Envenomed, I drink every drop; exsanguinating you, resuscitating my solitude.

Ambica Gossain

-Bittersweet fates-

We loved the only way we knew how, embroiled in constant turmoil.
For our hearts burned with passion and heat, craving the distaste of heartbroken defeat;
to relive what it was like before the dawn of the fights that darkened our days with the
quiet of the night.
We loved the only way we knew how.
Our love charred to hate and our hate sparred in defence of love
and somewhere in there snickered good old lust;
pirouetting lasciviously with our taped together trust.
Suspending it like a guillotine so very keen, to fuse our bloody hues, entwined in
bittersweet fates aligned.

~ We were always built differently. I, of all the things that fall apart and you, of all the
things that stay together.

Ambica Gossain

-My words-

My words, a thread I bead with rhyme and string together mellifluously with rhythm, ring insincere adorned with these embellishments.
Their essence stripped, entombed in an ornamental casket,
they shimmer like a bejeweled treasure chest of empty promises.
But I fear that without them, you may not accept them, nor find them attractive; thus rejecting me.
So perhaps they're best left six feet under this false pretence,
this mud I cake my face with everyday to belong.
Perhaps that's the only way to keep them alive; to speak within this silence.

Ambica Gossain

-Sanctuary-

I pushed them down and buried them deep;
my woes under the ground, for the earth to keep.
But when I opened my eyes, they were staring back at me;
my furrowed brow, their sanctuary.

Ambica Gossain

-HAPPINESS-

Happiness knocked on my door today,
but I wasn't too sure whether it was here to stay;
or simply to divert my attention long enough to whisk my words away.
So I stood there, armed with my pen, lest it try to convert me again,
consorting with misery, my perverted lifelong friend to rewrite my "happy" end.

AMBICA GOSSAIN

-FADE-

I don't care for journeys. I crave beautiful endings.
Doesn't matter what you said when I was alive, but what you'll do when I am gone.
I don't want you to break and drown yourself in tears but reminisce how I gave it all, so the life we chose didn't become the trap we didn't.
So the adoration I felt lingers on everything I touched.
So the dreams I contrived were as important as the ones I sacrificed.
For my soul to mean more than my body ever did; to be remembered with affection and not forgotten with regret.
Grant me this my love and I shall fade gracefully into the night.

AMBICA GOSSAIN

JAROD WABICK

[RODANDREW16]

Jarod Wabick is a Mental Health and Substance Abuse Counselor in Buffalo, NY. Jarod was raised in a Suburb of Buffalo. He has a Bachelors in Psychology and a Master's in Mental Health Counseling. Jarod has utilized writing as an outlet and coping skill since grade school. Jarod's style of writing has changed from short stories to song lyrics to poetry. When Jarod isn't working or writing he enjoys visiting antique shops, watching documentaries/movies/tv shows or reading various novels or books of poetry.

-Carnal-

the wind
caught
the edge of my
bottle
and
it made a howling
noise
so i
howled back
and
smiled at this
carnal moment
with
mother nature

JAROD WABICK

-Pretending-

I often wonder
what the
animals
think

of
us

as we
trounce
around

pretending

that we're
any
better

JAROD WABICK

-Exhale-

the earth
itself
has been holding
its breath
and
wincing

for some
four billion
years

and I am
patiently
waiting

for it to
exhale
and

breathe

JAROD WABICK

-Beautiful-

thought
about life
too hard
and

felt a rib
crack &
my nose started
to bleed

and as the
blood
trickled down
my beard

I smiled

because they
could
burn it all
down

and the
world
would still be

beautiful

JAROD WABICK

-PINT-

you can't really
fear
hell

when there's
a pint
glass

saved for
you

on the
shelf

JAROD WABICK

-CARCASS-

if I'm
quiet enough

I can
sometimes
hear
the vultures
in my
head

pickin' the
meat
off the bones
of
some of those

terrible
memories

JAROD WABICK

-Boa-

felt out
of
place

couldn't quite
fit
my body
into
the

universe

felt tight
on
my

bones

JAROD WABICK

-Fractured-

we shouldn't
have to
wake up each
morning

just to count
each &
every rib

to make sure
they weren't
busted

by the
weight

of
it
all

JAROD WABICK

-Lost-

the last generation
angrily
asks us
why we do
what
we do
and

we will
undoubtedly
ask the next
generation

why they do
what they
do

when the truth
is

no one knows
a goddamn
thing

sometimes not even
how to
smile

JAROD WABICK

-OutCast-

the bird out
there
on the wire
is
starin' at me
again

because he knows
I don't
belong here

that none of
us
do

and I know
it
too

but we both
stay silent
and

never speak a
word
of it

JAROD WABICK

-Fear-

i fear
being
understood

for i've
yet
to understand

myself

JAROD WABICK

-Knotted-

some do
not
want   to acknowledge

their brain   the
untangled   beauty

just some-   in
one   the
                              knots

JAROD WABICK

-BELIEFS-

i believe
in love

entirely

just not
entirely

in human-
kind

JAROD WABICK

-HUMANITY-

i yearn to
be
more monster
than

human

for the
former

is much more
kind &
understanding

JAROD WABICK

-Lookout-

i'm not asking
you
to go runnin'
covered in
warpaint
into the battle
that rages
inside
me

i'm asking
you
to watch
from some high
ridgeline

and just under-
stand
that it's
there

JAROD WABICK

-INERTIA-

I am
reaching
for
the various
molecules of
myself

that are
floating off
into
space

as I pull
apart

while i
try

to hold
myself
together

JAROD WABICK

-Knocking-

the chatter
in your
skull

gets loud
like
old machinery

and you start
to worry
if anyone
can hear

and sometimes
you
hope

that they
can

JAROD WABICK

-INTROSPECTION-

i sometimes
don't recognize
the
words
that have been
pounded in ink
on the paper

don't know
what depths of a monster
they came
from

and that's
when I know
they are
real

JAROD WABICK

-CORROSION-

life doesn't
change
all that much
over the
years

it just
burrows holes
in you

and then
the light
starts to filter
through
a little different

JAROD WABICK

-Resilience-

the most
resilient
parts
of my body

are the
ones

that cannot
be
carved and
cut out
of me

Jarod Wabick

-SONGBIRDS-

despite
everything

the birds out-
side

still sing

clenched to
branches
and

powerlines

and until it
all ends

so will the ones
in-
side
me

clenched to
my bones
and

powerlines

JAROD WABICK

-SEEKER-

i thought
maybe
if I sat
in the sun
long enough

some part
of my soul,

that I hadn't
yet
noticed,

might come
crawlin' out
my pores

and into
the light

JAROD WABICK

-Deliberate-

so much
of this
life

is on
accident

but tonight
I will
burn

on purpose

Jarod Wabick

-Gifter-

give the
world
art

when it
tries
to take

your
soul

Jarod Wabick

-Hyenas-

when you
start
to laugh

violently

and can't
stop

because
life

just is
and

the tragedies

just are
and

the past

just
was

JAROD WABICK

-PEARLS-

they will
try to
convince you

that you
must

always

show your
fangs

but you
don't

JAROD WABICK

-COMBUSTIBLE-

sometimes
you have to be
quiet
enough

to hear
the crackling
inside

of that
fire

that
still
burns

JAROD WABICK

-Fire Breather-

you can
be
kind to people
and they
often won't know
what to do
with it

they juggle it
around
in their hands
in their mouths
like a
hot
coal

but
please
be kind

until the world
is used to
the
burn

JAROD WABICK

-WILD-

yes

part of
you
is human

and the
rest

a million other
wild
creatures

JAROD WABICK

-Determination-

i noticed this
audacious
little flower
come swingin' up
through a crack
in the
driveway

or maybe he
cracked it
himself

and for the life
of me
I couldn't kill
him

and I felt more
like a man
than I ever
have

JAROD WABICK

-ABSORPTION-

i want
you
to recognize
the immense
breadth
of beauty
in it
all

to the point
that your
body
starts to hum
and
vibrate
and begs
to burst into
flames

JAROD WABICK

-ENERGY-

fill your
insides
with
the
universe

until your
skin
can no longer
hold it
all
in

JAROD WABICK

Julie Godfrey

[LOVELYLOGOPHILE]

Julie lives in Toronto where she is currently pursuing her Masters of Divinity in Theological Studies. She is a true romantic who lives life with arms wide open, absorbing every experience she can through the joyful pursuit of music, art, nature, literature, road trips and service to others. She writes for purely cathartic purposes and finds poetry the ultimate channel for her intense emotional nature. Though definitely an introvert, you would never mistake her for one for she loves engaging with others and has a warm, confident energy about her. She is thrilled to be included in this anthology and counts it as a surprising and wonderful blessing.

-BROTHER-

I'd absorb his pain
remove his witness
dehumanize him,
for love.

JULIE GODFREY

-ARBORIST-

A reach forward,
a tentative pressing into you.
With tender fingers I push into your soft warm chest
through your ribs
to the place where your heart hides.
I am alarmed - it's made of wood.
I press deeper, feeling its surface, tracing the ridges, looking for cracks or knots to
work my fingers into, to see whats inside.
There's no way in.
So I take my fingernail and tap, tap, tap, hoping to hear more
than my hope echo back
in hollow reverberations.

JULIE GODFREY

-SHIELD-

The tougher the man, the gentler I touch.
A soft hand, a soft word, a soft gaze
can melt iron towers into puddles of sweetwater.
The stronger the fortress
the more I know
the degree to which
whatever's inside is afraid.

JULIE GODFREY

-CELESTIAL RACKET-

I love you, please bother me.
Please derail my life of naive expectations with your ruinous divinity.
You are the perfect mix of dark marred soul and being of light.
You are my favourite interruption.
Crash into me.

JULIE GODFREY

-Mangle, Maim-

He held me softy,
so softly
as if I was a little bird.
But what I actually wanted
more than anything
was for him to crush my bones
into a billion fucking pieces.

Julie Godfrey

-Shock-

You were the wrong one, the wrong one, the right one.
I peered out into the light of day
I left you there, behind.
What have I done!
I forget
I remember
I remain.

Julie Godfrey

-Don't-

I never ask, "where are you going?" but
"where are you leaving me?"

JULIE GODFREY

-Entomb-

I run to you and start to dig
my fingers ripping into the ground
tearing handfuls of grass and dirt from the earth,
flinging them over my shoulder.
I made vows, Goddammit.
So I dig and I dig and I dig
until I'm covered in blood and snot and sweat and tears
because I will not rest until I pry open that lid.
I will not rest until I crawl inside and shut it tight behind us.
I said "'till death do us part" and I meant it.
I'm not living here without you.

JULIE GODFREY

-Chattel-

You say, "I don't want to lose you" and my heart leaps.
Then I remember: I never had you in equal measure.
I grasped for an ethereal you, smoke between my fingers,
and the unfairness breaks my heart.

JULIE GODFREY

-Lure-

He promised me a kiss
right over there by the bushes
so I ran barefoot across the moss and brambles
but he wasn't there.

He promised me another
in the hollow of that tree (the one hidden in the glen)
so I ran with bleeding feet
and broke my back to fit inside
but he wasn't there either.

Finally, he promised me THIS TIME a kiss
under that rock
off the shore of the lake, do you see?
So I dragged my bleeding and broken body
into the water
towards that rock
and down
down
down.
He was there.

JULIE GODFREY

-Sick Beguile-

I fight pain with pain.
So when the ache of you becomes to much to bear,
I bite my tongue until a flood of salt and iron runs down my throat.
I batter my ear drums until warm rivulets of blood flow down my face.
I pull fistfuls of hair until I feel them rip free from my scalp.
I tear off a nail
swallow boiling water
pay someone to hurt me
because all I want is the forgetting
of you
of us
of we-no-more.
So long as I savour
the blows, the jabs, the abuse,
the violence of this self-inflicted sort
I cannot feel the kind you serve up to me
against my will.

JULIE GODFREY

-Offering-

My friend once told me that as a result of childhood pneumonia,
his lungs had a small dead spot - it could be seen in his yearly X-rays.
I think if you took an image of my heart you'd see the same thing: a dead spot,
in that place where I loved you from.
Self-sacrifice.
A piece offered up to save the whole.

Julie Godfrey

-A Breaking-

I lifted my naked, too skinny body into the tub
slowly, carefully, gingerly and in reverse
(without the aid of my left leg, currently useless and terribly damaged).
"Will you wash my hair?" I asked, looking up at him.
"No" he said.
He told me it was too hard on him, seeing me this way: so weak, so vulnerable.
Somewhere inside of me, something broke.
I figured out how to wash my hair on my own, lifted myself back out of the tub and 2
years later
walked out the heavy front door
of our matrimonial home
and never went back.

Julie Godfrey

-Arrival-

The pain, the pain, I'd choose it again for I'd be less than perfection
were it not so.

Julie Godfrey

-An Emptying-

He's honing me
stripping me
separating me,
His loving fingers disentangling the ties that bind
(it hurts).
It feels like heavy
it feels like joy.
Like quiet.
Like raw.
I'm so, so tired.
He's setting me apart,
He knows what I'm made of:
I'm pieces of Him all rearranged in His fashion.
I know, I know,
I'm sure, I'm sure,
arise.

Julie Godfrey

-REVEL-

Haloed motes suspend in the dusk of eve
audible vibrations emitted from the vinyl cracking of a needle
uninhibited movements from bodies of children
worshippers
lovers;
my creatureliness delights.
More of this God, please.
More.

JULIE GODFREY

-INNOCENCE-

We turned our faces to the sky and gasped at the cold kisses the snowflakes peppered
on our faces.
In that moment we weren't our 40 year old selves, we were two children caught in the
splendour of pure joy.
Maybe the pain of your absence is so great because with you I wasn't just a woman,
I was a little girl too.

JULIE GODFREY

-HER-

I hear the tinkley little chimes from the back, the waaaaaay back of my truck
and the wayer back of my heart
her baby toy, from when I first met her.
When I left our home I took it, with few other things.
I didn't care about "the stuff", only the representations of our love. Of us.
Most of the time, I don't hear the chimes; this piece of her is snug back there against
other things.
But every once in awhile it breaks free and I hear it and think of her.
And love her.
And miss her.
I smile.
I cry.
There are things in this life I will never be able to reconcile, never be able to make
right, and that's ok.
Life is either about answering to or answering for and I have had to answer for this for
years.
If it means I get to keep her in my heart for one more "I'm sorry", it's ok.
I'll never be not sorry for leaving, even if it was to save myself.
I'll go to my deathbed sorry for leaving her.
I'm sorry
I'm sorry
I'm sorry.

JULIE GODFREY

-MOUSE'S BACK-

Do you ever feel like a colour? Today I am grey:
soft and somber
ethereal
thick.
Today I am pure grey.
Bones. Blood. Breath.
A melancholy whirlwind romance.

JULIE GODFREY

-THEN-

I thirst.
So I drink
and I drink
and I drink some more.
But it's never enough.
This unquenchable life destroying thirst isn't about _____,
it's my soul's desperate cry
from deep within the void
of the vast separation

from God.

JULIE GODFREY

-GOSSAMER-

I love being around the young young and the old old -
the veil is paper-thin around them;
one has just come from home
and the other is being beckoned back.

JULIE GODFREY

-HOLY-

It's 6am and I can hear the whizz, burr, buzz, scrape of the plows and salters coming to
rescue the early morning churchgoers.
It reminds me of when I was snowed in with you
when we tucked in a little deeper in my bed and you pulled me close to steal my
warmth.
Maybe you being gone is better.
Because why would I want to go to church when I can worship here with you!
(Wherever you are is where I'm closest to God).

JULIE GODFREY

-Influx-

I am 16 inches wide at my shoulders.
I am 74 inches tall, toes pointed.
My skin and muscle
and blood and bone
and fat and organs
and teeth and hair
and nails and breath
and my tiny little belly ring
weigh approximately 108 pounds.
I like numbers. They make me feel sure.
But how do numbers quantify existence?
What number equals the weight of my soul?
Can my spirit be weighed?
What about the memories that fill my head?
Or the feelings held in my heart?
Do my scars add weight or do they consume it?
When I am in love, and my eyes and my heart are bigger, do I weigh more? Am I taller?
And when the void of loss and grief come, am I smaller in my entirety? Do they shrink
me?
I am stretching this morning in the quiet, in my aloneness.
My skin is naked against the cool and I'm wondering these things.
I think my thoughts in the morning are always in their purest form.
I think I am indeed lighter in the morning.
How could I not be? Morning is rebirth.

Julie Godfrey

-DANCER-

I am an empire
form made from void
light, land, transient
and homeward bound.

JULIE GODFREY

-THE IN-BETWEEN-

I sit in the waiting room
first world hospital, clean, bright, expensive.
I'm talking to God, thinking about the what-ifs,
asking for the strength to endure whatever is coming (I hope it's easy).
Echoing down the hallway, faintly, a person sings.
Either from a stairwell or a bathroom,
I can't make out the words
only hearing sonorous notes
from a sterile chamber of resonance.
I wonder: is it a lament or a hymn?
Could be either in this place.
I choose not to return to my book
I'm being ministered to
I can feel it in my bones
and I'd just like to sit here awhile and forget.

JULIE GODFREY

-Mine-

My hands, they are my comforters, my communicators, prophetic emissaries.
They cover my face when I cry, alone.
They enwrap my ribs when I lament my state of affairs.
They stroke my hair when I am too sad to sleep.
They play guitar
know sign language
scribe my heart
feed me (when I let them)
and make my bed with clean sheets.
They petition and receive from The Father
move the Holy Spirit
comfort the grieving
hold the beloveds
and express my love with violent affection.
These hands, they are not "piano hands": long and languid and delicate.
They are boney and vascular and rough. I never thought I would love them.
But oh, do I love them.
Because the knowledge they impart to me, the power of the love they convey
can only be found in their touch.
And when they effortlessly find each other and grasp one another in their hold,
I am not alone.
I am mine.
I am so completely mine that it takes my breath away.

JULIE GODFREY

-Come in-

Tell the pain that's it's ok
tell it to pull up a chair
tell it to sit.
Ask it how it is
hold its hand
stay with it.
Stay with it.
Serve it tea
wrap it in a blanket.
cry with it.
Visit well.
The thing about pain is it just wants to know it's safe
wants to know it's not wrong
wants to know there's a place that is shaped exactly like it's own dimensions.
The thing about pain is all it ever wants
is a loving "welcome home".
Welcome home.

Julie Godfrey

-Blessed Traveler-

All this time I sought an other
all this time I assumed a walk alone, incomplete.
Now I realize the truth,
the thing of the thing that always was:
every part of this life I walk alone
every part of this dream
me, myself.
Solitary.
One.
And in this, freedom.

Julie Godfrey

ASHLEY MULLER

[VIA_WORDS]

Ashley Muller spent most of her life in Florida, where she grew up and graduated from Flagler College with her B.A. in Communication. Now, she has traveled west, and writes from her converted campervan, currently somewhere in California. Like many writers, Ashley began writing in journals and diaries at a young age. Her writing became a way to express the emotions she kept bottled up, after losing her mother to cancer when she was 9 years old. It became difficult for her to "talk" about her feelings, but with writing she could always find the right words. "I love the way humans can connect on some of life's most complicated feelings through a simple poem" she says. Ashley's favorite possession is her teal Erika German typewriter.

-Eclipse-

The moon is always full darling
As is my heart for you
It's just that some days
this world gets in the way,
It casts shadows over our light
But I'll still shine for you my dear
Morning, noon, and night

ASHLEY MULLER

-Waiting-

It was the kind of love
That stood right in front of you
Waiting
Waiting
Waiting
For you to sift through
All the others
that were never meant to last
Waiting
Waiting
Waiting
For you to realize,
I am the one.

ASHLEY MULLER

-Maybe Tomorrow-

Just remember that this world is always turning
And the moon is always pulling on our heart's strings
Playing with us like puppets
And the stars are shinning brighter certain days
And now just isn't the time for love

Ashley Muller

-Shooting Stars-

I watched
As the stars fell from the sky
And as I fell
back into your arms
A twinkle in your eyes
As things became aligned

I wished for this.

Ashley Muller

-DECEMBER-

Winter has me turned around
The sun is shining
But the flowers are dead

I am cold hearted
But comfortable
In the blanket of your arms

Tomorrow I'll be wanting summer
But tonight I want you

ASHLEY MULLER

-SUNKEN SHIPS-

I'm drowning in your love
Waves of unmet promises
And white-capped lies
I have sunk this ship a thousand times
And I will take it down again
But only this time
When we hit rock bottom
Our love will remain a treasure

ASHLEY MULLER

-Autumn-

I lay among the rotting leaves
As I watch the last one fall
Are we all doomed to feel this way?

Let the snow collect on my skin
Burry me in your winter
I swear I'll bloom again

Ashley Muller

-Pieces-

I'm falling apart
As every piece of me
slips right through my fingers
I am shattered , scattered
in a thousand scenes left unfinished.
Why does time only move forward,
When will it ever stop.
I question with every breathe
Will I ever be whole again?

Ashley Muller

-TOMORROW-

It was one of those days
You just didn't want to move
With each shift I felt heavier
Every time I tried to lift my head
I buried right back into the pillow
I've covered the windows,
Blacked out the sun
Not a crack of light will tempt me
Today is not my day.
But tomorrow,
Tomorrow I will try again.

ASHLEY MULLER

-FREEZING TEMPERATURES-

Don't act like the air hasn't changed
The sharp frigid stab of a winter breeze
Taking back every breath I held
Waiting for you

ASHLEY MULLER

-Remember the Time-

I tip-toe over black ice
Black ice,
Black ice,
That reminds me of you.
In fact,
Everything reminds me of you.

Ashley Muller

-Bleeding Hearts-

Oh, these flowers
they bloom in colors
that remind me of a girl I used to be.

Now, I'm just stuck in winter season.

Ashley Muller

-Wild-

The seasons are changing,
just like the paths laid out before us
I just hope that when I'm gone
You see my eyes in the twinkle of the stars
You feel my love in every setting sun
You hear my voice in the whisper of the wind,
& My dear, I just hope you remember me
As all things wild

Ashley Muller

-Daylight-

There it was
That twinkle of light
That came through the trees
Just as I made eye contact with the sky

It wraps its rays about my skin
And reminds me that
spring always comes after winter

ASHLEY MULLER

-New Day-

It felt as though
I had stepped out of the shadows,
Rays of light warmed against my skin
My sadness slipped away
And my writing became mute
There was nothing left to pour out in ink

I became my own sunshine

ASHLEY MULLER

-New Chapters-

A book store
Embedded between my bones
Each copy a collection of memories
Hidden between hardcovers
I trace my fingers down the spines,
As I wander through the silent shelves
Each story begging to be read again
I thumb through the pages of a life I once lived,
As I make space for a new chapter to begin.

Ashley Muller

-Sealed with a Kiss-

Love never dies
It gets put in an envelope
And filed away in my heart

It might not be here now,
On the skin between you and I

But I still remember the way you loved me

Ashley Muller

-TAKING BLAME-

& One day I realized
The only thing standing between
Me
And my happiness
Was me.

Ashley Muller

-SPRING-

My heart started blooming
like wildflowers in july
The sun blinding me
of the cold dark winter
you put me through

Ashley Muller

-ASHES-

I struck a match
And lit a fire in my soul
I burned all the memories I had of you
And my world became a brighter place

Ashley Muller

-FLOW-

hello, bright light of life
You've scared off the shadows
That were cast over my hope
I've decided now is the time to fight back against fear
And fall in love with myself all over again.
Isn't it funny how the times keep changing
And there's nothing we can do except go with the flow, smile & grow

ASHLEY MULLER

-SOULMATES-

I don't know you
But something in my soul
Recognizes something in yours
Like I've known you in another lifetime
& I'm so happy to have found you again.

ASHLEY MULLER

-AMONG ASPENS-

It's like everyone's an Aspen
And I'm just a pine
As they change with the wind
And the seasons
And they die
And I just stand here tall,
And weather the storms to come.

ASHLEY MULLER

-RAYS & REMINDERS-

The sun flickers on my lashes
Tickling my sight
Poking me in the side
Saying
"Hey you , don't forget your smile today"

ASHLEY MULLER

-Salvation Mountain-

Look no further than yourself
for the answers that you seek
are not in the sky, beyond the stars
rather they are deep
beneath your skin

Ashley Muller

-Soar-

Love is not a ball and chain,
It is staying up all night
Building you a set of wings
And pushing you off the highest peak

I don't want you to stand by my side
I want you to soar beyond this world you thought could keep you down.

Ashley Muller

-UNITE-

Can we all agree that it's time
To stop coming together to hate
And start coming together to love

ASHLEY MULLER

RHONDA SIMARD

[JUST26LITTLELETTERS]

Rhonda Simard lives in a small town in Northern California. She is a wife, mother of two sons, and elementary school teacher. In her free time she likes reading, writing, podcasts, crossword puzzles and cryptograms. She also enjoys yoga, bike riding, and nature. She has written and self-published a children's book called Moon Ladder. She has always enjoyed writing, playing with words, and rhyme.

-Letting Go-

They leave and return:
Tides, visiting distant shores
stealing and sharing grains of sand.
Echoes, words on wind,
wavering, but bouncing back.
Winds, whispering secrets
slowly shifting,
flurries or feathers on air.
Children, we hold tight
gripping tiny hands,
slowly releasing,
fingers crossed,
waving not goodbye,
but see you soon.

Rhonda Simard

-FIRESTORM-

Meandering through
change
Dust and ashes follow
flames
Rubble, scattered debris
hides a story there
and gone
Lost names.
Half of two lifetimes
Obliterated,
the other
relocated.
She roars,
her tears the only
rain.

RHONDA SIMARD

-SAND AND HOURGLASS-

Boulders loom, withstanding the ages,
while you spin out in the gravel.
Why go in if the mud's too thick?
Unfathomable the quicksand battle,
as you smile and put rocks in your pockets.
The inevitable rain will pour.
But you don't own a monopoly
on the tears
or pain or loss or hardship.
We all trip on the rubble,
scrape our knees and elbows.
Still you sit in a box
with a rock on top,
as the sand in the hourglass ticks.
Go lakeside, please,
find some stones to skip.

RHONDA SIMAR

-On Tiptoe-

A little girl, a yellow dress
peeking through a knothole.
Standing up on tippy toes,
One eye opened
one eye closed.
Though the grass is rarely greener
she longs to run, flying dress
through that maze that leads us
to the edge of wilderness.

RHONDA SIMARD

-The Ever After-

A cloudless sky
filled with fairy-tale magic,
sharing blues of wistful powder
soft to the touch.
Reaching only to grasp
silver linings that cut
from blue to shadow black
as darkness stalks to
swallow me up.
Hesitantly hoping
for fictional skies
while ever-afters
flood my eyes.

RHONDA SIMARD

-Starfall-

Tumbling tears
like falling stars
or drips on windowpanes
racing.
Origin   a black cloud
              a black hole,
Destination an   abyss
                      unknown.
And stopping them
is like trying to hold
water in cupped hands
or count stars one by one,
overflowing.

Rhonda Simard

-Just a Drop... or Two-

The leaving sinks me.
That hollow feeling...
Like trying, while crying
salty rivulets,
to empty an ocean
using a ladle.
Endless scooping
Fruitless
The droplets pool.
Wave goodbye
and try to camouflage
The outpouring.

Rhonda Simard

-A Sad Sea-

This dichotomy
as a sad sea
washes over me
pulls nails from finger beds
drips droplets on forehead. . .
and like lighting matches
to burn ashes,
Unfathomable.
Burnt fingertips
like swift kicks
to the stomach.
When I hurt already.
A closed book.
No lock, no key.
Just me.
Downtrodden
in darkness,
sad sea.

RHONDA SIMARD

-Baby Roses-

Peering through the nursery glass,
lined, like a rose garden,
little miracles
under the sunshine lights.
Pink roses come to mind.
New life, such promise
like buds they begin
Tender flesh, tiny toes,
and fingers like flower petals reaching.
I feel my heart fill my chest, pounding
As I ponder
seeds, stems, growth,
Life.
Magical.
Little systems modeled after
larger versions
before the thorns.
Not capable of worry
they simply grow.
It's time to go,
like leaving the womb,
farewell field of roses,
beautiful by design,
Bloom.

RHONDA SIMARD

-Bird's Eye View-

Tears fall,
It's gravity.
Simply grave, and not so simple.
Looking down at the world
from on high.
Very few get an aerial view,
that green and brown patchwork quilt.
The rest of us earthbound
fitting pieces
into the puzzle.
A mosaic
this life.
May you soar. . .

Rhonda Simard

-Birds and Bees-

Flowered sundress lifted
Spring weather and
gentle hands caress
curves and valleys.
Butterfly kisses and
lips sipping nectar
reaching deep in
delicate petals.
A flush, a burst, the bloom.
Amid the wildflowers
hearts beat breathlessly
and dreams incubate.

Rhonda Simard

-A Million Little Things-

When life is a winding road
and your heart is carsick,
like trying to keep a lake between shores,
Friendship
Stands on water's edge, skipping stones.
As easy as breathing in,
baby ducks,
butterflies,
and birdsong.
As hopeful as starlight
after an orange horizon,
stolen from the sky.
Golden giggles,
warm soul.

RHONDA SIMARD

-Flames-

Feeling the world on fire.
Metaphorically and for real.
Smile heavy,
Stare steady,
As flames incubate
before they explode.
The current state of things
bewildering.
Bright-eyed optimist,
trying not to frown,
Control freak
trying to keep
the world from
burning down.

RHONDA SIMARD

-ANGEL-

Forgotten. Alone.
The wind blows
leaves like confetti whispers
through her garden home.
The breeze tickles
her chipped marble wings.
Ants scurry across her
worn alabaster
in and out of her tiny nose.
Black mildew
creases formerly ivory crevices
time erodes tiny lips and toes.
Now a fallen angel
everlasting, fashioned from stone,
weather-worn and weary
All alone.

RHONDA SIMARD

-SOFT SHOULDER-

The hurt squeezes
like fog's icy fingers
a vice,
hard angles, rough edges,
splinters, burns and ice.
Is it too much to ask
for some softness?
Tender flutters of butterfly kisses
from eyelashes blinking,
snowflakes winking,
and delicate confetti sprinkling
like sifted flour and flower petals.
The gloom and doom
is not leaving room
for bubbles. . .
Iridescent and giggling
high on stardust and daisies,
calm breezes and babies,
snug blankets to fend off the cold
a shoulder or a warm hand to hold.
Feline belly fur, and purr
padded paw prints, soundless but sure
and gentle.
Like silent prayers
slightly leaning toward
a miracle whisper cure.

RHONDA SIMARD

-Son One-

Sailing along in his sturdy vessel,
A pirate of sorts, with his sea legs
and saltwater smile.
An ocean home
bleached shores its lacy skirt.
Expansive vastness masking
life left behind. . .
Like dropping anchor
expecting to catch it,
grasping madly while knowing
it is going
to the depths
with no hope of return.

Rhonda Simard

-An Unravelling-

Early echo, "Hang on tight. . ."
Chubby hands gripping braided cable,
fearless falling,
dust-knuckled flight.
Joyful swinging, clutching line
Eyes closed spinning
on twisted twine.
Reverse, a dizzy unfurl
backwards breeze meets sunny day
Time passes, ropes burn
and stretched-thin fibers fray
in tug-of-wars
real and imagined,
this dangling to and fro. . .
Untying a knot
that's become a noose
free to breathe,
coming loose. . .
letting go.

Rhonda Simard

-Wildflower-

She, a wildflower quilt
freely scattered,
edges unsewn,
seeking safety from
confinement,
locked basement.
Alone.
Hiding from sun
opening downturned eyes,
blinking silken petals
blooming,
searching pastel skies.

Rhonda Simard

-A Christening-

My head swims
The vast scheme of things bewildering
An unfathomable river
I lean closer. . . eavesdropping.
Witness the water   whispering
                              shouting
                              crying
                              laughing
Living
She is simply on another adventure, journeying.
The rocks and jagged corners still snag us
                              tug at us
                              slow us down
But the stream shoulders her spirit, singing.
My head swims
A deluge over my cheeks
A waterfall
Cascading.
I scoop up her soul, splash my face,
And take her with me.

RHONDA SIMARD

-Drifting Leaves-

A thief
like a leaf on breeze
snatches my creations,
pilfers pieces of me
like winter stealing the sun.
This holding on
means letting go.
A mountain withstands
the elements,
though crumbling some.
A frozen lake,
afraid to break,
is still a perfect puddle.
Memory laden tears fall
like raindrops tugged from eaves
brown to green
child to teen
then free to rise, to fly
to drift to another location.
The leaving a piece of the cycle,
like stolen snowflakes,
they are leaves on breeze.

Rhonda Simard

-Lost Seasons-

As my ice begins to thaw,
your river returns to the sea.
Shivering, I search for you,
hoping you will search for me.
Your rainbow shines in the distance,
my colors dance and sing.
My winter exhales its closing breath,
and searches for your spring.

-Upward Bound-

RHONDA SIMARD

We
and the trees
gather in parallel lines
deeply rooted though cloud-bound
a skyward climb
limb by limb, breathing in
our ousted air.
Exhaling life-breath, they share
holding nests with care
simply soaring through blue
touching stars on black
storms brew. . . lightning strikes. . . we crack. . .
We. . . fall
(even if there's no one to hear at all)
All at once sturdy and
bending in breeze.
Eternally losing leaves,
We
and the trees.

RHONDA SIMARD

-Poetic License-

Sea surf surges
waves whisper, roar and echo
as we crave to be heard.
Leaves litter the forest floor
as we hide, our mask a dappled disguise.
Desert wind rages eternal
stealing life with sharp bony fingers
as we, pen in hand, fear being erased
like faded ink on paper.

Rhonda Simard

-A Winding Road-

Navigating this maze,
this trail less traveled,
takes careful footwork.
We are all winding roads
and back alleys,
more complicated than the parts
in which we were cast
in someone else's play.
The script like trying to cross
a cracking, splintered bridge
barefoot past boneyards
and icy detours
slippery when wet.
Safe travels, wayfarers. . .
Embrace the forks in the road,
steer your story,
pilot your poem.

Rhonda Simard

-ROOTS AND WINGS-

Looking back.

Recalling stories,
wives' tales, warnings
of childbirth, fear.
Pain, of course, but no tears,
until my little miracles appeared.
Years later, and they are falling again,
by the bucketful.
Our umbilical cord cut twice,
once when they arrive,
and once when they fly.
The last of my little miracles
waves to go
turns with no

Looking back.

RHONDA SIMARD

-GOODBYE SONG-

Soul mirrored in a darkened river,
As sunset steals the light, I shiver.
Her current steady, eternal, strong,
Sings an endless goodbye song.
On the banks alone, my torn heart grieves
She whispers hope, but forever leaves.

RHONDA SIMARD

-BUDDLEIA-

Silent, a lonely island
in the solitary blue
as flitting butterflies
flutter
blooming flowers, social glue.
Alone, but not lonely,
a purple-blossomed bush
full sun, but casting shade.
Soundlessly sharing
in the petal dust and glimmer,
this treasured island
blooms and fades.

RHONDA SIMARD

-Behind Closed Doors-

Cleaning up another's mess,
literally and figuratively,
risky business.
Blowing cobwebs from mementos,
trash and treasure equal parts.
Breathing storied dust
into voyeuristic lungs
and heavy heart.
Intruding
as opened drawers whisper secrets
that can't hide
in an uninhabited room.
Exit, shadowed gloom,
and lock clicks,
Stowing memories
in cardboard boxes,
lights out,
heartsick.

Rhonda Simard

MEI RYAN

[LIPSTICKANDMIRACLES]

Mei savours the sacred in the everyday and writes poetry that celebrates simple miracles. Ever since she was a child, she has had a deep affinity for words and writing. Her love of travel and nature also inspires many of her poems.

Mei's poetry has been featured in the San Pedro River Review (Fall 2017 issue) and on literary ezines like Literary Juice and The Connotation Press. Her work has also been nominated for The Pushcart Prize. She posts micropoems regularly on her Instagram page, @lipstickandmiracles.

-ACCEPTANCE-

These hands have tried to shape rocks
and pleat oceans into husk
Whittle "Be brave, be strong"
into a shiny pill
Because I'm told a tame heart is sick
Women must rise
Grasp the moon and whip the wind.
But there is room in this world
for the midnight jasmine
hushed new snow
and my glasswing nature.

MEI YAN

-EVERGLOW-

all I ever wanted
was to belong
to the everglow
of slumbering
sunsets and the
brave sweep of
haughty winds
feel one with
their invisible
hearts beating
in step with mine.

MEI YAN

-Moments I-

Day undresses slowly peeling
off corn-blue skins sacred
dance purple glazed and fired in gold.
Setting sun trails
deep red ribbon
across a willing horizon
before yielding to the dark.
Whole cycle of
breathlessness. We
intoxicate ourselves
mirror-dusted
on that Indian summer night
oiled only with a full drop
of fragrant moon.

Mei Yan

-Moments II-

Waves caper like fish
ten million trout-blue bellies
pregnant and emptied by turns
in summer noon.
Slide against uneven white face
tempting songless rocks
to melt slowly
into the sea's indigo trance.
We send white-sailed wishes
into the pink shell-scented wind.
The message laughs back
in glass-blown waves around us,
this moment like every other
is perfectly shaped.

Mei Yan

-WAKING-

Lemon slice waxes
a slow spreading sea anemone
in black honey tea.
Scent of pink hyacinths
salts thin glass edge.
Unexpected morning wraps itself
around familiar flutter of fear.
I surface to the sound of full white tulips
releasing petals.

MEI YAN

-COLLECTING SEA STORIES-

Carried by moon-drawn crests
we touched and told stories.
Pieces of gold scattered
across our Mediterranean Sea,
green with laughter and
speck-salted memories.
With only strung words
holding burnt sun in tandem.
Voices washed clean
across titian shore,
moored white shells
awaiting passing ears.

MEI YAN

-Winter Hours-

Join me in the slow fade
When moon rise suspends
As if a pale ballerina poised on pine tips
Waiting for the sleepy beetle to roll away his kingdom
While wild geese and lovers take the long way home.
Join me in the quiet hour
When all the little creatures know we are loved.

Mei Yan

-Matinée Ensoleillée-

Morning spread before us
Like a forest feast
Gleaming with dreams
Still heavy with stardust
Laced with the scent of moon and
Your arm on the crescent of my waist
This winter light that rushes in
Leaves no heat
But oh what gifts of hope it brings
For another day with you.

Mei Yan

-Jeunesse Dorée-

Before I go, let me
dip my wings in gold
from the morning sea
Soft summer nectars
from the amber fields
kindled by young love
From the gentle daisy
turned heaven-ward.
With these wings I'll fly
to the end of the world
where whatever waits
I'll touch with my gold.

MEI YAN

-One Shine-

Oh the yearning wind said
Don't let these days disappear
Hold on to the wavering sun
All the shine she's gathered
Let them spill over the shiver
Walk tall through the salty pine
But lean gently against the memories
Feel the past wash over like a song
Carrying us across the clean blue fire.

MEI YAN

-WALK ON MY LOVE-

Everything moves so memory may form
Walk on, my love.
We may be dumbfounded by the forward charge of our lives
These feet that carry us into the night
The warmth that races through our veins
To fire an empty heart.
Walk on, my love.
Trust the soft earth
And the wind
We are one with the ever-changing.

MEI YAN

-19 SEPTEMBER 2017-

Rest, my wandering mind
Close the miles between our
feverish possibilities and the
silent waves of this moment
We don't have to choose.
Let the sea and forest melt together
They are all light after all.

MEI YAN

-Slow Ways-

Ours was a joy
Forged in the slow ways
Of feeling every blinding moment of life's passing
In the wild ways of hearts breaking
Mending, rebirthing
A joy hard-earned
And now, well-spent.

MEI YAN

-Adrift-

After the fall
We thought we could piece together
memory
Stitch sunsets to the scent of snow
Bind the sound of love to everything
Make whole a
moment
That time has splintered
Our choices ravelled so carelessly
That nothing keeps us
moored.

MEI YAN

-Journey-

I want to go far away
Farther than I can measure
Press my distance against the world.
Until bird calls become unfamiliar and
The wind brings me scents I cannot name.
Until nothing is left of me but the journey
This one night under the shooting stars.

MEI YAN

-Sakura Hour-

There will be seasons of devastation
when the body is barren,
No amount of love will make her bloom
and she might forget that
she is one with the sweet, blue grass.
But when the sakura hour comes —
And come it will —
All the bright things call her by name.

MEI YAN

-SO NONE MAY LEAVE-

We search the dark for signs of grief
Implore the sky so none may leave
The tears that run come swiftly sweet
Stacked against the silence we meet.

The stolen storm brings no reprieve
We know that such is life so brief
Our love like thorns returns to greet
Stacked against the silence we meet.

MEI YAN

-THERE ARE FORESTS IN THE SKY-

My heart is like a broken loom
It can weave only one life at a time.
I choose the one of still forests and quiet brooks
(without you).
Every ~~precious~~ possibility of us
I bury deep in an unfamiliar sky
Where nothing laid to rest ever grows.

MEI YAN

-YIN YANG-

Did you think the seasons marched in single file
Winter the sequel to Fall's foibles?
The truth is they coexist at every moment —
Regard the changing leaves flaming with August sun
Spring folded into quiet bright wings
The sleeping earth cradling daffodils under the snow.

Did you think there were chambers to separate
The sweetness of the Tunga River from the
Bitter balsam you hold at the back of your tongue?
Let me tell you, they coexist at every moment —
Every joy mourns the passing of time
Every grief is already dressed in hope.

MEI YAN

-BUILDING BRIDGES-

Life is long
That bone-splitting heartbreak
Nursed in moonlight till it gleams blue
Will be one of many pebbles in your ivory stream
Someday you'll look back and see a step-stone bridge
Know those moments offered an opportunity
To journey to yourself.

MEI YAN

-DRIPSTONE HEART-

You know that time has passed
When your once smooth heart becomes
A jagged terrain of winding rivers and warm valleys
Silent caves and cloud forests
A mysterious, beautiful land formed by
Every ray of light you were thankful for
Every precious tear that ran its course slowly.
S l o w l y.
Your dripstone heart is how
You know that time has passed, and you have lived fully.

MEI YAN

-SEASON OF REST-

We forage the winter
For warm, happy endings
Robe the pondering branches
With twinkling reminders of joy
As if they were our own tired bones
In need of cover from a season of rest.

Let's celebrate instead
The stillness of waiting trees
Let them be stark and withered
Let wind and snow make their home
They don't need to be beautiful all the time
Love grows strong even in the quiet of sunless days.

MEI YAN

-METAMORPHOSIS-

Like the caterpillar, we must know when
To retreat into our silken wisdom and
Spin ourselves into a hallowed silence
It may be frightening when we reach out
And touch the smooth back of loneliness
Feed on moonlight dust for days while the
Wind tempts us with the scent of masses
Yet my sweet raconteuse, persist we must
If we are to be goddesses of our own truths.

MEI YAN

-STORY OF BLACK BIRD-

The black bird and I
Recognised each other
We had a long chat
About the wild things
The quiet, dark things
In the forest that have
No names, no place
No stormy resolution.
"Don't disown them",
He said, "Hold them
dear so they may be free."

MEI YAN

-Open Heart-

Is your heart open
to let in thunderstorms
Soft curves of moonlight
and salt-laced winds from
warm seas that carry roots
between us in search of
fertile lands where joy
will grow in every season?

MEI YAN

-Meditation on the Shore-

I heard you this morning
in the cloud song and sea sighs,
telling me to let go now.
"Melt into the pull of the silver moon
Come with your simple breath and broken praise
Leave everything else by the water's edge
Neatly folded and blessed.
Jump into the fear and flow.
Swim into the joy and flow.
Just flow."

MEI YAN

-DEAR YOU-

Go quiet and sure towards moonsongs
Towards the traceless flight of a million birds
Seek trophies of moments wrapped in light
Cherish the meeting of transient souls who leave nothing behind
Stay in invisible pauses between desire and strive
In the miracle of you - here - in this world.

MEI YAN

FAY LEE

[THESTUBBORNPOET]

Fay Lee is a writer of poetry and flash fiction; her work was awarded Recommended Writer in the 2nd Quarter London Independent Story Prize (2018) and one of her poems was longlisted for the Fish Poetry Prize (2018). Fay has recently begun sharing her work on Instagram; @thestubbornpoet.

-BLOODY LOVE-

Bloody love
here we go off and up like a rocket so
fast impatient to get to the place we
want to be next. Raging
love, like a bull running up to the
flag desperate to reach the red without
knowing what lies
in its hues.
Rolling fast, playing games on a
patch of dead grass, unseeing the mess
that we tread with our heavy souls.
Stupid love, feckless and reckless and
naively forgetful. Cold and old.
And more often than not
entirely mis-sold.
Bloody love.

FAY LEE

-Splendour-

I see you
I touch your skin
could it be my
skin you're in?
Look at you,
lit with splendour.
Hopefully,
the best of me
while not all you see
will be
all that you remember.

Look at you,
Lit with splendour
Hopefully,
the best of me
while not all you see
will be
all that you remember.

Fay Lee

-Clear-

I can feel the heat of your cool
blue eyes
on my skin.
Your gaze makes me
hide, makes me wriggle and
giggle.
You see all that's within
me
but you love
and you want
regardless of shade or scar or
creased tissue.
You look at me and all at once I become
completely undone.
Yet,
you still look at me
full of calm,
like you wagered it all
and you won.
I wonder if I'll ever see what you do
through those eyes bold and clear
and be as sure about me
as you.

Fay Lee

-ONCE-

Remember,
when we would play
together? The freedom
of the sunshine weather
the days that seemed
to drift on
forever.
Remember,
When everything was
fine! When I was yours
and you were mine
how we laughed together
how we danced in
time.
Remember,
when we talked all
night! Ourselves and our
secrets tucked in tight
our safe tiny
world being just
right.

FAY LEE

-BUTTERCUP-

We sat underneath a buttercup moon
Whispered goodbyes that
came lifetimes too soon
One skin, one moment, heart
thudding to heart
Knowing the future meant
being apart.

I sit underneath a shy first sun
Warmed by memories of where
we begun
I knew you then I know
you now
It will have to be enough.
Somehow.

FAY LEE

-FAR-

Apart
is too far
for my
trepidatious heart.

FAY LEE

-STRINGS-

Invisible
strings must
connect us because
I can still feel
You

FAY LEE

-DUST-

Take my words.
Breathe them in.
Taste them
and see how they feel inside
your skin.
I'd prefer you
to take what you need
from afar while you read
and leave me for dust
without me feeling
a thing.

FAY LEE

-EXHALE-

I wish I could let it drop
Lightly
Gracefully.
Let it drift, leaf-like
to wherever it
happens to go
and to not need to know
where it lands.

FAY LEE

-SURE THING-

You know the thing about
the sun and the thing
about the rain
is that they have no
prejudice, they fall
on us the same.

And whether we wish they
would stay or go they
grace us just the same
there's nothing more forgiving
than drops of sun
and drops of rain.

FAY LEE

-Now-

No matter how many times
I close my eyes in wish
or how mightily I strive to
summon up the memory.
It is never the same
as falling into the arms
that made my pain fade fast
and relieved the claws
that live in my aching chest.
Those arms that were
my shelter.
And as
time both flies and
lurches on
it does not heal.
It reveals.
And in its unfolding
it teaches me
that I will never go home
again.

FAY LEE

-Yesterday-

Yesterday, I though of
all of the trees that are perfect
for climbing up or swinging from, for
engraving endearments into eons
old bark.

I thought of all of the streams
that were perfect for paper
boats or catching little fish, with
slippery, smooth stepping stones
waiting for exploring feet.

I thought of how nature nurtures
adventure and wondered how many
perfect, pure playgrounds are paused,
noiseless and undiscovered.

So,
we are going out to play.
Today.

Fay Lee

-BLISS-

The milky moon leads me
along a winding path
a velvet sky envelopes me
in a navy starlit bath.

I drift across the highland
bare feet tracing bend and curve
I know that I am safe here as
clouds cushion worn out nerves.

I long for you to swallow me
to feel a comet's kiss
to drop into your dark blue hues
and give in to the night, what bliss.

FAY LEE

-Ceramist-

She sits with this
feeling. Rolls it around in her hands
such precious dough.
She warms it and brings it
to life.
Her palms breathing air
giving wings to a moment
of simple wonder.
She feels you in the clay.
It flows through her
fingers so the curves
she creates
match the gap you left
in the place where you lay
when you went away.
A cold unyielding
blends into
such beautiful softness,
a natural remaking.
Her hands, giving motion
to feelings that need solid shape.
Sweet creation flows boldly from this
wild tenderness.
A longing
to know that something remarkable
could become
of this splendid mess.

FAY LEE

-WAIT-

In the weightlessness of freedom
in the lightness of choice,
through the colours of hidden rainbows
under the power of a voice.

I do not need to seek it, it sits
in wait for me.
A thousand joyful moments that I
can reach
and feel
and see.

FAY LEE

-QUIET-

When the sun
Hits the hills or
Folds pinkly into the sea
When morning rises slowly
Into the stillness of
Deep sleep
When the night cloaks over
Familiar shapes of distraction
When the stars stand still.

This is where you wait
Peace
Is where I find you.

FAY LEE

-FREE-

When the person who holds
your heart, knows everything and
can trace your skin onto paper.
Can read your mind with their eyes.
When they know the parts of
of you
that are the secrets
you keep from
everyone else,
it is a different kind of freedom.
A divine acceptance.

FAY LEE

-CONSENT-

This body
Each mark
Every curve
All freckles
Each smile
Every fold
All openings
Each closing
My heart
Each wrinkle
Every line.
It's
all
MINE

FAY LEE

-BULLIES DOWN TO A T-

Their torturous tongues transform to tin tipped teeth then
their tricky truth tears tender tissue to tatters.
They tell tall tales, they twist them troublesomely tight,
till talk transcends truism, turning the tangibility tide.
The traitorous tallyman tracks tabs too towering to top,
teary targets trail, tougher than they thought.

Today's tourney through.

Triumph the tomorrows.

FAY LEE

-SHE-

Rumbling
tumbling deep down
in a part of me
unreachable and free,
I feel the pull
of the tide gather
pace with each breath. You
can't fake this feeling it's there
or it ain't.
Oh, and it's great!
It's fearless it's strong it feels so
at home it could never be wrong.
I know I belong.
I am that wave.

We are the sea.
Connected by currents and swells
older than time.
Femininity.
Together. It's yours and it's mine.
It's our potent
potion,
concocted of eons of loving devotion.

There's nothing mightier than this ocean.

Sisters
Sisters are awesome
such beautiful acceptance
invincible love. . .

FAY LEE

-It Stays-

Time refuses to stand
still, a whole calendar
year
has staggered by without you
near.

Like the stoic seedling that
shoots up through every
season
Like the much-missed friend
who turns up without a
reason
Like the majestic seas choose
to bless the same old
bays

You are there
You wait
Your love
                    It stays

FAY LEE

-Alphabetty-

My veins are full of letters
every heartbeat rhyming rapture
my stomach is aflutter with
words I long to capture
an alphabetic garden roots
in my flower bed
vowels and consonants skate artfully
on thin ice in my head
my fingers twitch with verses
poems course down to my toes
I'm top-to-bottom
inside-out
one hundred per
cent
prose.

Fay Lee

-Pals-

If time with you were a colour it
would be palest pink, with marbled swirls
of silver and spots of golden ink.
If time with you was a sound it
would be heartfelt laughter, the kind
you feel deep in your soul that
hurts your tummy after.
If time with you were a taste it
would be toffee sweet, with hidden
bits of zingy rum that surprise you
as you eat.
If time with you was a feeling it
would be quiet calm, with occasional
elation and lovely happy charm

Fay Lee

-BEAUTIFULLY BRAVE-

Being brave is beautiful,
it splits clouds and light trickles in, it reminds us
why we exist on earth
it makes us weep while we grin.
It 'beams us up scotty' to places, we never knew
we'd reach, it discovers new worlds
and creatures, it pens a memorialised speech.
It takes us away from our comforts
and lets our feelings out, it helps us be heard
by our audience, without the need to shout.
It tears down ignorance does bravery, it helps us
see the way, it ousts the liars and the cheats, it
comes to save the day.
Being brave is beautiful,
it ignites something in our bellies, it makes us
proud of our race when
we see it on phones and tellies, we see it
and we repeat it, braveness feeds the brave, and the hearts
that hold it keep passing it on even from their graves.
Some have it from when they're born, each step they take
is bold, but they pass it to others fleetingly
and let them have a hold. Take the chance when it's your turn,
to do what it is you wish to do,
take your courage and cast it wide, you'll be
beautifully brave
when you do.

FAY LEE

LIES DE WILDE

LIZZYINWORDS

Lies De Wilde is a singer and writer who lives in Antwerp, Belgium. Through 'Lizzy in words' she takes you on a journey through her life, how she perceives and experiences it through mind, heart, body and soul. Writing to her is a way of letting go and coping with strong feelings and emotions, which sometimes cannot be said out loud.

-Breakable-

I am the sensitive kind
the one who feels more deeply
who gives with all she has
I am the one with a heart full of scars
stitched together and torn apart
my love is made of the finest glass
it can last a lifetime or be shattered apart
treat with caution, handle with care
once broken, never quite fixed
I am the sensitive kind
the one who is stitched

LIZZY IN WORDS

-Mosaic-

She:
'how can you love me, with all my brokenness?'

He:
'my love, to me you are not broken
but like a mosaic put together with the utmost delicacy
filled with gold, what you call scars, because that is where your wisdom lies
what you call fragile, I call strong
I am in admiration of the uniqueness you possess
your love could tame the wildest seas, for many storms you've weathered
beautiful, not broken
that is what you are to me'

LIZZY IN WORDS

-I LOVE YOU-

I could tell you that I love you
but would you then truly see
how the world trembles beneath my feet
every time you look at me
or how my heart skips a beat
and my lungs withhold my breath
when your lips speak my name
and all clarity leaves my head
so tell me
would it make you see the same
if 'I love you' was all I said

LIZZY IN WORDS

-BREATHLESSLY ENAMOURED-

breathless did it leave him
to see the light that escaped the scars upon her soul
breathlessly enamoured to call this woman home

LIZZY IN WORDS

-MASK-

his eyes weren't fooled by the mask she wore
they looked into the essence, the depths of her soul
determined to reveal the beauty seen inside
and lay to rest her tormented heart

LIZZY IN WORDS

-FALLING LEAVES-

tears flowed as memories unravelled
his fingers untangling her hair
rain tapping on the window
almost soothing in a way
days were passing like falling leaves
one after the other, slowly losing colour
but right there in his embrace she knew
that no matter how much her tree would wither
or her colours would change
he would always be with her
like her memories
embraced

LIZZY IN WORDS

-The Maze-

it's a peculiar thing
that world inside my mind
a maze made out of roses
where imagination runs wild
with one prick of a thorn
nightmares can come to life
so prudence is required
where every rose has its own story
a land beyond all dreams
lifetimes could be spend in here
so be careful where you're led
within the maze inside my head

Lizzy in words

-Rivers dark as night-

fields of flowers blooming
along a lake of shimmering gold
but something dark was looming
behind the trees, inside the woods
a river growing dark and cold
as the years went by
a world of beauty and suffering
were both intertwined
and all of this lies hidden
in the depths behind her eyes

Lizzy in words

-SECRETS-

as flowers fell into a slumber
and closed their petals for the night
slowly she'd awaken
to share her secrets with the dark
for darkness could not see
and so could never tell
of the secrets she unveiled
that dawn would hide so well

LIZZY IN WORDS

-GARDEN OF DREAMS-

I walk in the gardens of my dreams
where secrets hide, a veil unlifted
the purest of places, the safest haven
here I sing my song, a siren's call
until you find your way back home

LIZZY IN WORDS

-LABYRINTH-

the labyrinth of time has been laid out before me
my melancholic mind travels through it slowly
in search of magic and adventure far beyond this world
let me drift and wander in search of something more
that one thing without a name
I cannot seem to find
for what words could explain what is missing in my heart

LIZZY IN WORDS

-OCEAN OF LIFE-

life is like an ocean
depths still undiscovered
secrets hidden in the dark
always moving, making its way
through time
whether still there or not
leaving its mark

some days tumultuous, others calm
memories long forgotten somewhere far beneath
until they wash ashore
revealing damage or beauty laid bare
reminding us once more..

LIZZY IN WORDS

-REGRETS-

I wanted to write you
but did not know what to say.
For how do you speak to someone
who takes your breath away.
Now I regret what's left unspoken.
That I can't turn back time.
So now, my love you live your life
and I'll try to live mine.

LIZZY IN WORDS

-TIPPING THE SCALES-

living at an imbalance
became a familiarity
giving more than what's received
can only last so long
at some point it is time to breathe
to rise out of these drowning waters
reaching for the sun
bask in glory, tip the scales
for once say no and change the story
feel the strength that is reborn
even if that road is lonely
see where it can go

LIZZY IN WORDS

-Preserved-

roses are bleeding and trees are weeping
as she exhaled her last breath
her body lain down in the valley of sorrow
where for eternity she would be sleeping
as snow covered her flesh
like a blanket of comfort
spring would cover her in flowers
like a memory preserved
As all endings have new beginnings
for there is life after death

LIZZY IN WORDS

-The way Home-

you are searching for things
this world does not have to offer
look beyond this world
and tell me what you see
would you still let the darkness
take your soul from thee
or would you turn to the light
the world and home of our Father
for He and He alone can save you
from your demons
unless you like the burning fires
that rip apart your soul
don't you think it's time
you finally came home

LIZZY IN WORDS

-Land of Wonder-

My love,
do you not see
the magic underneath your feet
open your eyes so you can perceive
how you have been created
you lost your way, a dimming light
blinded by the world
to the truth you hold inside
your essence pure and powerful
there in silence waiting

My love,
I feel that you are searching
for somewhere to belong
unaware that all you need
is already within
take my hand and I will fight
the shadows that you see
there is no darkness light can't conquer
and mine is shining bright

My love,
you'll find a veil has lifted
for the light that, in your eyes, I find
will finally roam free
together walking side by side
in a blissful golden glow
then you will know where you belong
Who you are meant to be

and the magic of this world
will be a part of you, eternally

Lizzy in words

-Leap-

at the edge of new beginnings
that is where she stood
the biggest fears unfolding before the final step
whispers of doubt still filling her head
yet one voice was stronger, feeding a flame
'jump my love for you are not a tree,
though you have roots you are also free'
a voice giving courage where none had been

drawing her closer to who she longed to be
and so a journey began and the edge of the unknown
held no more fear for me

Lizzy in words

-Nature's Fragrance-

howling wolves in the deepest of the night
nature shimmers under the gleam of starlight
the path of life lightened by the moon
knowing it'll be morning soon

and as the night turns into day
the sun chases away the grey
flowers fold open their leaves
while birds enchant you with melodies

the beating of my heart runs like the stream of the river
with every rock a new obstacle in sight
a shadow in the distance slightly makes me shiver
but somehow I know that it's all right

I can feel the earth beneath my feet
while questions make my head unclear
where will this path go, where will it lead
will it take me far away from fear

over mountains and valleys
I'm surrounded by its sent
nature's fragrance only leads me
where dreams never went

Lizzy in words

-NEW BEGINNINGS-

between the mountains
underneath the starry sky
they lay there silently, fingers entwined
as the lives around them were lain to ash
and the dust had settled down
they lay in the midst of desolation
and as the morning sun arose
bathing them in a golden glow
there was one task left that day
to build the world anew
out of darkness and destruction
into a glorious creation

LIZZY IN WORDS

-THE DARK-

am I but a creature of the night
am I nothing more to you
I too crave love and light
just like mere mortals do

I am where the secrets dwell
where darkness has no name
the cracks are where your light gets in
so all is not in vain

for I too wish to feel the sun linger on my skin
to have something like you so pure
so darkness cannot win

LIZZY IN WORDS

-FROZEN MEMORIES-

what is frost if not nature preserving its beauty under a thin coat of ice
trying to hold on just a little longer before the thaw takes it away
like old memories making room for new ones to come
blossoming into new beginnings

LIZZY IN WORDS

-SOUND OF SILENCE-

the water cleansed her
like a river flooding the wastelands
carried by the current while the eagles soared
high above on the waves of the wind
floating under water
where all the world was still
until she washed up at the shore
and the world, it became louder
with the ebbing of the sea
until silence was no more
the loss of her tranquillity

LIZZY IN WORDS

-POCKET OF FLESH-

even though she wandered
she was mighty and unafraid
for hope did not make her weak
and love, it was the instigator
of her warrior heart
carried inside a flesh made pocket
right there in her chest
beating with a steady pace
she set out into the world
you see a heart so full of hope and love
could set it all ablaze
the frozen lakes of captured hearts
to free where dreams were left to ponder
melting fires fed by wonder

LIZZY IN WORDS

-THE WOLF-

take me into the wilderness of your world
where the night sky is filled with stars
and nature is untouched
take me into sunsets on the sound of beating drums
where mountains are kings that rule up high
where you are home and your heart is free
into the wilderness
walk with me

LIZZY IN WORDS

-Valley of Souls-

she was born into a world ruled by egos
a world where she was out of place
and so she set sail on a journey
like a hummingbird is search of nectar
to find a land where her soul could be free

travelling across the wildest waters
guided by the stars
there towards the misty mountains
she heard crying from afar

cries that to her ears would sing
of long forgotten memories
a call of nature so pure and bright
an awakening of senses luring her in

until she reached a valley of flowers
with colours beyond what the eyes could behold
beings of light, shimmers of wings
living in peace, a place she'd fit in

a frequency more high and serene
vibrating through every fibre
a home for the soul to roam wild and free
the place I belong
my Home is with Thee

LIZZY IN WORDS

-VALHALLA-

I've walked over frozen lakes and snowy mountains
I've weathered many storms in search for Valhalla
and when I crossed the misty valley in search for shelter and a roaring fire
I found Valhalla in your arms

LIZZY IN WORDS

-MICHAEL-

I can rage like the thunder with the impact of a hurricane
but when you wrap your wings around me, I find peace
like the sky after a cloudburst
the garden inside me starts to bloom
and I, I am at ease

LIZZY IN WORDS

-Listen-

have you ever stopped to listen to the humming of the earth
or wondered how the wind is trapped beneath the wings of a bird
have you ever truly seen the beauty in a waking flower
or in the tapestry of dew drops glistening beneath the sun
have you taken the time to feel the vibrations of the universe
to feel the energy surrounding you
the glorious light emphasising your celestial worth
then,
have you truly never wondered how we deserve the earth

Lizzy in words

-Twilight-

come meet me where the wildflowers grow
where the sunlight warms my skin
I'll be waiting here upon the meadow
till twilight's sinking in

Lizzy in words

ANNE RYAN DEMPSEY

[ANNESPAROW]

Anne Ryan Dempsey grew up near the ocean in Coastal Virginia, where she now teaches writing and literature. She loves nature, and often draws her inspiration from images she has seen from her travels across the United States and around the world. Anne enjoys reading, art, photography. She is passionate about kindness, compassion, listening to others' stories, helping others, and animal rescue and welfare. Above all, Anne hopes to fuse grace, love, and beauty into her writing. You can follow her work on Instagram @annesparow.

-The Desert-

i think sometimes that
i am the desert.
& nothing alive can survive in me.
i choke back 1,000 tears
(but there is no water)
& all of my words are turned
to ash.
where's the rain?
where's the rain?
(it's coming; they say)
& so i will take the next step,
& the next one.
& i will learn to
bloom from ash until it
rains again.

ANNE RYAN DEMPSEY

-THE ALCHEMIST-

i tell you that i'm afraid
to take these thorns from my
side, (for they have hidden the
ache for far too long)
you hold my sadness in your arms,
collect my tears in a bottle
(you count every one that falls)
& like an alchemist, you melt
my leaden tears to gold,
(& they soften the thorns where they fall)

ANNE RYAN DEMPSEY

-THE WINTER BEACH-

we walk the winter beach
(the wind is ice &
the water glows emerald-blue-beyond)
the gulls shine silver & i stop my stride:
hundreds of broken shells—
fragments of a former life
(orchid, opal, moonstone, linen)
tumble in the tide
are washed new in the tide when i realize
there is hope for the broken things.

ANNE RYAN DEMPSEY

-Not Afraid Anymore-

i was a girl who liked to hide.
behind walls, behind people, behind the frost
that smothered the wildflower's breath
because i was afraid.
& one day, a prism of light
flickered onto my palm;
it swayed & stained a rainbow
onto my skin & suddenly,
i was drenched
in color & fire
in opal & flame
in phoenix songs & glory
i saw. i saw that
all i was hiding was my light
(& i had spent too much time afraid of a shadow)
when a flame cannot hold darkness at all
i am not afraid anymore.

ANNE RYAN DEMPSEY

-Tropical Road-

when i am lost &
(when the sadness sits on my heart;
when the waves of grief wash over my heart);
i find this place,
this tropical road,
where the sapphire-flamed birds nestle
(into the palm of God)
where the tigers are my friends &
we are safe. we are safe.
we are beautiful.

Anne Ryan Dempsey

-Sparrow-

i lay my head down in a garden of stars
& accept that sometimes the
sparrows don't sing
(but i can hear the frost whisper
hope to the dirt):
"all will be new";
"all will be new."

Anne Ryan Dempsey

-BLOOM-

there is magic in the dirt where you bury fear.
magic in the dirt where you bury fear.
in the dirt where you bury fear.
where you bury fear
you bury fear
(bloom).

ANNE RYAN DEMPSEY

-METAMORPHOSIS-

scatter my identity beneath the dirt;
let it sing unseen with winter roots;
let it stretch into pale blossoms to live, &
then, (lay me among the dying petals)
& here i will bloom again.

ANNE RYAN DEMPSEY

-The Storm-

a storm stealthy creeps;
cloaked clouds & slate
streams of snow--
the sky boils fury &
you are afraid, but
wrapped in a blanket of stars,
another day will crawl
from beneath the ice &
the sun will suffocate fear
(love will overcome fear)
& you are held
by the Light.

ANNE RYAN DEMPSEY

-Thick Skin-

i have given up on growing thick skin,
(for i want to feel the ocean soak my bones);
i want to feel the colors that don't exist;
(i want to feel it all)
& i know people will hurt me, but
(there is a meadow on my sleeve)
& it will bloom anyway.

ANNE RYAN DEMPSEY

-A Rebuttal-

someone once said to me:
"you are too gentle for this world, too soft—
a flower to be crushed with the weight of
wilderness."
but—
"kindness is the wild in me—
softness is the strength of a thousand seas.
i will bloom for joy
& astonish the world with color.
as for the terrible world—
that's why i stay soft."

ANNE RYAN DEMPSEY

-My Body-

let my body be a safe place;
let it be (a home).
my arms are strong to
cradle life;
my hands can
feed the hungry;
my hands can warm
the cold.
forests can grow from my
fingertips if i plant
a seed.
let my lips
speak the language of butterflies
that have kissed the sky for the first
time.
let my shoulders carry hope
for others.
let my body be a safe place;
let it be (a home).

ANNE RYAN DEMPSEY

-A Love Story-

& you, you make it all better.
you stepped into my darkness &
(wove the stars into my hair)
you said there is glitter
in these bones &
(kissed the fire in my skin.)
you smile the light of 100 suns
and i will never be cold again.

ANNE RYAN DEMPSEY

-Roses in Cement-

love is busy
in the abandoned places
(in the frozen places)
planting roses in the dark
(growing roses from cement)

ANNE RYAN DEMPSEY

-BRANCHES-

we are all branches
of the same tree
(& some of us are)
digging for stardust in our pockets
to scatter through the night.

ANNE RYAN DEMPSEY

-DON'T STAY-

wildflower, listen—
don't stay.
don't stay in a place
where you can't feel the sun.

ANNE RYAN DEMPSEY

-THE MOON'S MAGIC-

the moon's magic
is her resilience
to bloom through the bleak
she gives her strength to the dark
but always burns back brighter.

ANNE RYAN DEMPSEY

-The Healing-

& this about the healing;
(it will come)
(it will come)
there is no agenda for it.
it will reach you;
let it take its time;
be patient with yourself.
let it arrive with the everglow
of a harvest sunrise;
let the breeze wrap around your shoulders
& taste the warmth of the light;
(let it trickle in the hurting places)
& trust—
it will happen,
(the healing)
in this life (or the next)—
the leaves die every year,
(& they are not afraid)

ANNE RYAN DEMPSEY

-Winter Rose-

to the winter rose
(all ruby & milk)
that holds the heavy snow—
(your bare arms tremble)
you carry so much;
it's okay to let go.

Anne Ryan Dempsey

-Fall Softly-

let them all fall softly.
the things that are hard.
the things that are heavy.
the things that are hurting.
let them all
f
a
l
l
softly

Anne Ryan Dempsey

-BLACKBIRD-

to the blackbird
singing fragile hope
to turquoise stars,
do not give up.
tonight could be the night that
you move the universe.

ANNE RYAN DEMPSEY

-SLOWLY-

do not be afraid to go slowly.
even the moon
(who carries time on silver shoulders knows)
she cannot be made whole
in one night.

ANNE RYAN DEMPSEY

-PROMISE ME THAT-

i hope that
when you look in the
mirror you see
a garden growing from
every place you thought
was a flaw.
i hope that you see
starlight painted inside of
your bones
i hope that you see wings rising from
where the pain used to be
(i hope that you see everything you are is magic)

ANNE RYAN DEMPSEY

-One Day-

here, have this hope—
step into it & pull it up
around your shoulders, reach back
& draw the zipper. hem it up
with starlight & stitch out the seeds
until they bloom wild roses
everywhere, everywhere.
now, wear it—
wear it on the day you will dance,
dance over your pain,
dance for the redemption
you know will come,
one day.

ANNE RYAN DEMPSEY

-ON A MONARCH'S WINGS-

it's magic out there now
the tree lights drip frozen glitter
& so i clasp my hand over my heart to treasure
wonder, thrill, grace;
(i clasp my hand over my heart to carry
a promise for tomorrow)—
hope lifted on a monarch's wings into an azure sky.

ANNE RYAN DEMPSEY

-IMAGINE-

imagine that God, he sings over you
(a lion's roar, a lion's song)
bury your sorrow in his copper mane
(& courage will bloom; courage will bloom)
his wings will wash your icy tears
(& spring will arise; spring will arise)
the cherry trees climb from a frozen death
(& all will be new; all will be new)
death will die when he sings over me
(songs of a wild, glittering hope) —
"your best days are yet to come;
your best days are yet to come."

ANNE RYAN DEMPSEY

-AUTHOR INFORMATION PAGE-

As always, we at A.B.Baird Publishing believe that all our writers are incredibly talented and encourage you to explore new writers often! To see more from the authors in this anthology, please us the information below to find them on their social media platforms.

Ambica Gossain	Instagram- @tryst_with_fiction
Anne Ryan Dempsey	Instagram- @annesparow
Ashley Muller	Instagram- @via_words
Fay Lee	Instagram- @thestubbornpoet
Jarod Wabick	Instagram- @RodAndrew16
Julie Godfrey	Instagram- @lovelylogophile Twitter- @lovelylogophile
Lies De Wilde	Instagram- @lizzyinwords Facebook- @lizzyinwords
Mei Yan	Instagram- @lipstickandmiracles
Rhonda Simard	Instagram- @just26littleletters

Dear Readers,

Our goals here at A.B.Baird Publishing center on continuing to empower writers by giving social media based authors as many avenues as possible towards publication. If you are interested in how you can become published, or want to stay up to date on our latest ventures, please join our email list on our website www.abbairdpublishing.com or visit us on instagram @a.b.baird_publishing.

Your reviews mean more to us than you realize! One of the keys to continued success is having reviews on sites such as Amazon. If you have enjoyed this anthology we ask that you please let us know by leaving reviews on the amazon listing. In addition we always encourage you to check out the authors on their social media accounts and let them know what you think of their work!

Thank you for your support- without you, we would be nothing!

Austie Baird – Owner
A.B.Baird Publishing